FACING ZIKLAG

Turning Crisis into Crowns

KIM M. MAAS

A Ten35 Productions Publication

kimmaas.com

Layout and Design by Sabrina Schlesinger Graphic Design
Cover Artwork by Sabrina Schlesinger Graphic Design

Printed in the United States of America

Part I
Facing Ziklag

Introduction

There are times when a great intensity in the Spirit is present: a powerful pressure in a transitional moment just at the beginning of a shift. Often in those times, it feels on the inside like everything is different and yet on the outside everything is still the same. That is the most frustrating part. It is as though a shift has happened in heaven but has not yet manifested in daily life. There is a waiting, a watching and the feeling of intense pressure – like being nine-months pregnant. When nine months pregnant, you feel large, clumsy and uncomfortable. You do not sleep well and find it difficult to rest. You just wish this baby would come!

Some of you feel like that right now.

Sometimes, our journey toward destiny is not easy. Sometimes, somewhere in between, we come to a place where it feels just a little too long, a little too dark, a little too hard, and a little too scary. Yet in those moments the Holy Spirit comes along, takes our hand and says, "Just keep swimming. Just keep swimming."[1] Well, maybe that is another fish tale, but the Holy Spirit loves to encourage us on the journey.

Not long ago, this is where I found myself. It had been a long season of transition full of emotionally heavy, physically, and mentally difficult circumstances. I was emotionally, mentally,

---

[1] https://movies.disney.com/finding-nemo, accessed July 7, 2018.

physically and spiritually drained. I felt very tired. I had lots of unanswered questions. The Lord was teaching me a whole new level of endurance and dependence on Him. Amid these circumstances, abruptly, there came unexpected events I could not have anticipated. The enemy was in my face daring me to rollover, give up, step back, lie down, and walk away from my call. I refused. I would not turn back. I would "Just keep swimming."

Where I found help for this very difficult time was in 1 Samuel 30.

Let's pray:

Lord Jesus, release a spirit of encouragement over this reader. Let there come, Lord God, a restoration of hope, confidence and courage to stay in the journey. Release fresh hope that this journey will come to an end in glory, in your presence, and all the best is yet to come. We will not be disappointed. So I pray for this word sent forth and I'm asking, Father God, that you would make room in our hearts for more; that our hearts would be good soil for the seed to be planted, and the seed would not be stolen, choked out or displaced but it would bear a harvest of good fruit so that we all will finish well. May we be made able to stand with Paul and say that I ran the race for the prize of the upward call and finished well. All Glory to God in Jesus name, Amen.

I Samuel 30: 1-9, 18-20

"Now when David and his men came to Ziklag on the third day, the Amalekites had made a raid against the Negeb and against Ziklag. They had overcome Ziklag and burned it with fire and taken captive the women and all who were in it, both small and great. They killed no one, but carried them off and went their way. And when David and his men came to the city, they found it burned with fire, and their wives and sons and daughters taken captive. Then David and the people who were with him raised their voices and wept until they had no more strength to weep. David's two wives also had been taken captive, Ahinoam of Jezreel and Abigail the widow of Nabal of Carmel. And David was greatly distressed, for the people spoke of stoning him, because all the people were bitter in soul, each for his sons and daughters. But David strengthened himself in the Lord his God. And David said to Abiathar the priest, the son of Ahimelech, 'Bring me the ephod.' So Abiathar brought the ephod to David. And David inquired of the Lord, 'Shall I pursue after this band? Shall I overtake them?' He answered him, 'Pursue, for you shall surely overtake and shall surely rescue.' So David set out, and the six hundred men who were with him, and they came to the brook Besor ....

And David struck them down from twilight until the evening of the next day, and not a man of them escaped, except four hundred young men, who mounted camels and fled. David recovered all that the Amalekites had taken, and David rescued his two wives. Nothing was missing, whether small or great, sons or daughters, spoil or anything that had been taken. David brought back all. David also captured all the flocks and herds, and the people drove the livestock before him, and said, 'This is David's spoil'."

Background

Backgrounds are important to every story. They help us understand the story in its own context so that we can interpret what is going on correctly. The Bible is a true story. Context is important.

1 and 2 Samuel were originally one book. Samuel is a book about transition. Historically it was a time of great socio-political and religious shifting. Theologically, the book of Samuel reveals: (1) God's sovereignty, (2) His ability to protect His anointed ones, (3) His ability to bring about great reversals to fulfill His word. Great reversals are one of the running themes we find throughout the entire Bible.

The story of Jesus Christ is the greatest reversal of all time. God came in the flesh to save his oppressed and enslaved people and overcame the works of darkness. Esther is another example of a story of great reversal. Esther was an orphan who became Queen and saved her people. Joseph is another. His brothers threw him into a pit and sold him into slavery. Yet, he became the second most powerful person in all of Egypt, sustaining his people through famine. Think about Moses, Daniel, Peter, Paul and David. All stories of great reversal.

David is the primary character in the book of Samuel. The story is about David's journey from overlooked shepherd boy to promised, prophesied, celebrated King of Israel. He is God's anointed, living at the very center of a transitional time. He is a type of Christ. His life, his choices, his identity, and his calling are all intertwined with the transition happening in history.

By the time we reach Chapter 30, we are chagrined to find that David has spent the last five years of his life as a fugitive. While a fugitive, David built an army of mighty men, raided the enemies of Israel, and gained not only experience, but also territory, goods and renown (mostly among Israel's enemies).

Enter the events at Ziklag – the most pivotal moment in David's life before he is crowned king. It is twelve days before every obstacle is removed. Twelve days before he is crowned king. His decisions at this pivotal moment are crucial to the outcome.

> *It is twelve days before every obstacle is removed between him and his prophesied destiny. Twelve days before the great reversal. Twelve days before he is crowned king. His decisions at this pivotal moment are crucial to the outcome.*

At that very moment, twelve days before the great reversal, the enemy hits David hard and close to home. Throughout scripture, in times of transition just before the fulfillment of prophesied promises the enemy often brings a countermove. He designs a type of Ziklag for God's people. He seeks to wear us out, wear us down and turn us back. John 10:10 says, "The thief only comes to kill, steal and destroy". He wants us to believe we are forsaken by God and do not have what it takes to finish the journey. He wants us to believe the promises will never come to pass.

Yet Hebrews 10:35-39 exhorts us:

> "Therefore do not throw away your confidence, which has a great reward. For you have need of endurance, so that when you have done the will of God you may receive what is promised. For, yet a little while, and the coming one will come and will not delay; but my righteous one shall live by faith, and if he shrinks back, my soul has no pleasure in him. But we are not of those who shrink back and are destroyed, but of those who have faith and preserve their souls."

From Genesis to Revelations, God speaks a revelatory word to his people, his people receive it, and a time of testing ensues before the fulfillment arrives. The enemy always comes to challenge the word and with it, our faith, trust, and confidence in the one who gave it. The key to enduring until the fulfillment of God's promise is a confident trust in who God is and what He has said. Enduring to the fulfillment of the promise is the rich reward of confidence.

In Ziklag moments, the enemy comes to kill, steal and destroy confidence in God and his word so God's people do not endure and receive the fulfillment of the promise. But the writer of Hebrews declares we are not those who shrink back and bolsters this claim with chapter 11, the hall of faith. By faith Abraham went, by faith Sarah bore, by faith Noah built.

> "And what more shall I say? For time would fail me to tell of Gideon, Barak, Samson, Jephthah, of David and Samuel and the prophets, who through faith conquered kingdoms, enforced justice, obtained promises, stopped the mouths of lions, quenched the power of fire, escaped the edge of the sword, were made strong out of weakness, became mighty in war, put armies to flight." Hebrews 11:32-34.

Each faced great challenges yet endured to receive the fulfillment of the promises given by God. What is the point? This is faith. Faith chooses to believe God's word to the end in spite of the cost and the risk. Faith hears, responds and moves forward trusting God and His word through testing and trial until the promise is fulfilled.

Like David, we, as the people of God, have a part to play in history. The decisions we make as we face our Ziklag moments will make all the difference in the world for our lives and the lives of those who follow us; our children, friends, and those who are looking to us from afar to see how to live this Christian life of faith.

David's choices, his unwavering faith revealed by his response at Ziklag, allowed the power of God's word to be released bringing God's plan for his life to fullness. He endured and received the promise. He became the promised, prophesied King. The crisis gave way to a crown.

> "Blessed is the man who remains steadfast under trial, for when he has stood the test he will receive the crown of life, which God has promised to those who love him." James 1:12.

The question we face in our time is not whether we will face our own Ziklag, because we will. The question is, will we endure in faith until we receive the promise – until the crisis becomes a crown?

The question we face in this hour is not whether we will face our own Ziklag, because we will. The question is, will we endure in faith until we receive the promise – until the crisis becomes a crown?

The Third day

The book of Samuel is what we call a historical narrative. A historical narrative is a factual story not simply a list of facts. The author, inspired by the Holy Spirit, is writing to convey meaning to his readers. Everything recorded has been recorded in a particular way to give particular meaning to the narrative. The words are arranged to make an impact. The story, and each recorded part, has a specific point.

> "Now when David and his men came to Ziklag on the third day . . ." 1 Samuel 1:1a.

Notice the timing – *on the third day.*

Still bearing the stress of navigating an intense political situation with the Philistines, David and his men had walked 75 miles over three days on foot to get home. They had narrowly escaped. Imagine their situation. They have been carrying their weapons, provisions, and personal gear for 75 miles and for three days. Their supplies were low, their feet hurt, their hearts were in need of a place to let down. David and his men were looking forward to being home. They were looking forward to a time to rest and recover. Ziklag is their home away from home. They have been on the run for five years. They have made a home at Ziklag. Their wives, sons and daughters are there.

Scripture is emphasizing the timing of David having to face Ziklag; after five long years of injustice, after a long march and a harrowing political contest. The timing magnifies the intensity of the situation. David and his men are vulnerable and unsuspecting.

The Amalekites

". . . the Amalekites had made a raid against the Negeb and against Ziklag." (Verse 1b).

The Amalekites are the perpetrators. David has been raiding Israel's enemies, which included the Amalekites. It would be easy to see this as a simple retaliation. However, to get the fullness of this revelation we must go back to 1 Samuel 15. Saul is the reigning king of Israel. The kingdom is taken away from Saul and given to David by The Lord (though the actual transaction has not been fulfilled to this point) because he disobeyed God. Saul's disobedience caused him to lose his crown. What was his disobedience? The Lord told him to destroy the Amalekites and he did not obey the Lord's command. He left some alive.

Therefore, the Amalekites, who attack David at Ziklag, are still in the land. David was reaping the results of someone else's disobedience to the Lord.

> "They [Amalekites] had overcome Ziklag and burned it with fire and taken captive the women and all who were in it, both small and great. . . . And when David and his men came to the city, they found it burned with fire, and their wives and sons and daughters taken captive. . . . David's two wives also had been taken captive, Ahinoam of Jezreel and Abigail the widow of Nabal of Carmel." (Verses 2-5).

It Was a Very Personal Loss.

David and his men came home to houses burned to the ground. Their sons and daughters and wives gone – taken captive. David, though the anointed one, the leader, and the prophesied king, was not exempt. His wives and his children were gone too. His home also burned down. No one was untouched by the tragedy.

What Do We Learn from These Points?

We learn several things.

We learn no one is exempt from a Ziklag. It is part of the human experience. It is part of the Christian experience. I do not know where we got the idea that when we come to Jesus we no longer suffer. Receiving Jesus is not like taking a magic pill. I also do not know when we got the idea that if we pray all the right prayers and do all the right warfare we will avoid suffering. Peter says that we are not to be surprised or think it strange when a fiery trial comes to *test you*. We don't get to take that to God and say that's just not fair. It's part of the human experience. Being anointed by God, being the leader, being in ministry, and doing God's work does not mean we are exempt from the experience of tragedy and loss.

We learn that Ziklags are an attack of the enemy designed with you in mind. Satan is a real foe. We have a real enemy. He is not sovereign. He is not equal to God. Yet, he does have power and he does devise attacks against the children of God. We learn we are in a real war.

My Ziklag

We learn that Ziklags never come at a good or convenient time. The enemy waits until we are vulnerable. We don't see them coming because we are focused elsewhere. The enemy designs them to take you beyond what you can bear and take you out of the race – for good. Why would he send an attack at a time when you are well-rested and strong? No, he waits until you have been dealing with an ongoing work or family situation, a physical illness or some other draining long-term situation.

For nineteen years, I had been following the call of God according to a prophetic word and promise spoken to me. The last three years had been some of the most physically, emotionally, mentally and spiritually draining of my life. I was a full time senior executive pastor, full time doctoral student, wife, mother of three and grandmother of five. I was creating a women's organization, mentoring several emerging leaders, overseeing a prophetic community, speaking at a few conferences, making time for my husband, my children, my friends, and babysitting the grandkids a couple times a month. On top of all of this, I was dealing with my mom's late stage cancer, helping whenever I could. Just two weeks before the night I am about to describe, I had spent several nights in the hospital at her bedside after one of her major surgeries. I was tired, drained, vulnerable, and stretched to my limit. I was three weeks behind on my doctoral dissertation and deadlines of all kinds were pressing in.

One night, I drove from the graduation of one of my emerging leaders and arrived at a 40th birthday party for a friend and congregant. It was so good to have some down time. I was talking with a group of friends. I began to share some of the encouraging signs that marked the previous year and gave me hope that fulfillment of a significant prophetic word over my life was about to come to pass. In the middle of a sentence, I felt searing heat and pain fill the back of my head.

It took me to the floor within seconds. I was writhing on the ground, hands gripping my head, moaning and crying out in pain. I was rushed to the hospital where doctors were sure I was experiencing a burst aneurysm in the brain (which is deadly). In a flurry of doctors and nurses, I was given medication, fluids, and a battery of tests such as MRI's, CT Scans, and spinal taps. For a week I lay in the hospital in intense pain and agony. I finally returned home weak and wearied. The tests found nothing. The doctors could not find a reason for the pain in my head. My own Ziklag – a specially designed countermove of the enemy to take me through a trial at a vulnerable time in my life – beyond my own strength to cope.

I spent eight weeks recovering. To this day I am not sure how I wrote the last 120 pages of my dissertation in that time. Ziklags never come at a convenient time.

We also learn that sometimes the enemy brings a Ziklag through the open door of someone else's disobedience or bad choices. This is challenging. The temptation is to get stuck on the injustice of it. We cannot get stuck here. If we get stuck on the injustice of the circumstances or get caught up with needing to assign blame rather than dealing with the issue, we will not get through our Ziklag. It may be true that someone didn't do what they were supposed to do, made bad choices, and caused us harm. It isn't fair. In that moment we must remember, we are not responsible for what they have done, but we are responsible for how we respond. How we respond is the outcome of our choices in any given situation. The choices we make in those difficult moments reveals our faith and moves us closer to or further away from God and his purposes for our lives.

> *We are not responsible for what they have done, but we are responsible for how we respond. How we respond is the outcome of our choices in any given situation. The choices we make in those difficult moments reveals our faith and moves us closer to or further away from God and his purposes for our lives.*

Lastly, and most importantly, we learn that Ziklags are designed to dismantle our faith and unravel our confidence just before a breakthrough or a great reversal.

David's Mighty Men

"And David was greatly distressed, for the people spoke of stoning him, because all the people were bitter in soul, each for his sons and daughters." (Verse 6).

All the people spoke of stoning him. Who were all the people?

Earlier, the Scripture stated the Amalekites took everyone captive, leaving no one. Who then are all the people? This passage is talking about David's mighty men. When they saw the devastation of their homes and found no dead bodies they knew the enemy had taken their wives, sons and daughters captive; a fate worse than death. It meant for them a life of slavery and abuse at the hands of their enemies. It was more than the mighty men could bear.

In their Ziklag moment they became *bitter in soul* and turned against David. Why would scripture point out their bitterness? Let's look at 1 Samuel 22:2 again:

"And everyone who was in distress, and everyone who was in debt, and everyone who was bitter in soul, gathered to him. And he became commander over them."

David's mighty men, in their Ziklag moment, lost sight of their future and regressed back into their past, becoming again what they once were – bitter in soul. They chose the familiar over the promise. In their grief and despair, they let go of what they had believed – the prophecy and promises of God regarding David. They let go of their kingdom identity as King David's mighty men and could not find a way to hope in God. They reverted to their old selves – bitter, discontented, grumbling, angry men.

Bitterness of heart and soul affects our judgment. It causes us to turn on those we love and who love us. It causes us to turn away from the call of God on our lives. This is the goal of the enemy. He is challenging everything we believe about God and ourselves. This is nothing new. The serpent did it to Adam in the garden when he questioned him. Did God really say? Are you really a defender of this garden? Don't you think you should have more power? Here, why don't you eat this apple!

From the beginning, the battle has always been over who God is and what he has said. Our identity is in Christ. If the enemy can strike at the core of our identity and get us to succumb to a lie, we will walk away from who we really are and the call that is on our life. We become angry and bitter at God, blaming and judging and turning from Him. The enemy *never* fights fair.

> *From the beginning, the battle has always been over who God is and what he has said. Our identity is in Christ. If the enemy can strike at the core of our identity and get us to succumb to a lie, we will walk away from who we really are and the call that is on our life.*

David's men were mighty men of valor, but they became bitter and discontented once again. In their anger and grief, they judged David, blamed him and began to threaten him. They threatened their friend, their leader, their prophesied King.

I have mentored several young people through the years. There was one young man that I poured into whose life was a mess from the harsh circumstances of his life. He began to change and soften. His countenance became so clear and clean. He started to step into his identity. It was then he faced his own personal Ziklag. It was a breakup with a girlfriend. She said some very unkind things to him in that moment. He could not let go of what was said and forgive her. It caused bitterness of soul. He turned away from all he had learned, the call on his life, and the God he was trusting. To this day, he has not returned. He could not believe and trust God in the Ziklag moment. He could not find the strength within to go on. So, he stopped and turned back.

David Grieved

David's response to all that was happening reflects his choices and his faith. There are four responses for us to consider.

> "Then David and the people who were with him raised their voices and wept until they had no more strength to weep." (Verse 4)

First, David grieved with his people.

He was authentic and not religious about his present experience. David felt pain. He was the leader, yet he sat among his people and wept until he had no more strength. He did not deny his feelings or pretend that he was unaffected by the loss and tragedy in his life. Sometimes we get tired. Sometimes we experience suffering and loss as fathers, mothers, pastors, leaders, and Christians. There is nothing worse than a plastic Christian who spiritualizes everything and can't be honest about pain. David was not ashamed of his feelings. He grieved over his losses. He grieved so intensely it drained every ounce of his physical strength. He grieved until he was finished grieving. He grieved among the people. He grieved as one of them.

When my mom was diagnosed with cancer, it was a very difficult and painful time for me. Even before she died I was sad and sometimes I would experience intense grief. It would come and go as it pleased. I did not get to choose the time and place. I am a Pastor and leader in the body of Christ and I go to God for comfort, but sometimes the grief would visit me unexpectedly, in the pulpit, in front of people; those who knew me well and those who did not. I had to choose whether I would allow myself to grieve and feel the pain – even if it meant the public exposure of my heart. I chose not only to trust God, but also the body of Christ. Though I am a leader, I am a part of the body. I need the Body of Christ to comfort me, pray for me, and stand with me in hard times. I needed it during that time.

Emotions are not ungodly. They have a place in our humanness. Denying emotions is not Christian; it is unhealthy. For so long, Christians have equated emotion with a lack of faith. This is just not true and it has produced a plastic caricature of Christianity that denies the human experience. At the same time, we do not live by our emotions. We live by faith. We must learn how to deal with emotions, to experience them without allowing them to lead. In other words, our feelings do not lead us. Our feelings do not direct our choices. Living by our emotions will cause us to react rather than respond.

One day, many years ago, when I faced a crisis in my life and ministry, I learned a very hard lesson. I found myself caught up in the politics of church leadership that had gone sour. It was my first staff position and I was very green. The emotions were intense everywhere. In the end, I was unable to navigate the situation wisely, made some wrong choices and stepped away from my post very disillusioned. Over the next two years God began to heal me. In prayer one day, He said to me this one important thing that has become an anchor for me ever since. He said, "Kim, I don't want you to act out of your emotions anymore. I want you to respond with wisdom." I was astonished. I had had no experience with a situation like that before. I realized I had been caught up in the politics that were not about me. It happened because I became emotional. I realized in that moment I had been led by my emotions. I could suddenly recognize that some of the things I said and did added to that whole confusing mess. I left the position feeling it was all someone else's fault, but when I had healed enough the Lord spoke to me revealing my own part. He said, "I do not want you to ever do that again". And I never have. I have never again reacted out of my emotions rather than responding out of wisdom. I experience my feelings, but I am not led by them.

> *We must learn how to deal with emotions, to experience them without allowing them to lead. In other words, our feelings do not lead us. Our feelings do not direct our choices. Living by our emotions will cause us to react rather than respond.*

We must be people who are authentic about our emotions. When we need to weep, we must weep. We are not above suffering and pain as Christians or leaders. Learn to grieve well. Again, emotion is part of the human experience.

Just as emotions are not to lead us by directing our decisions, our emotions must not become an identity.

When an emotion becomes an identity, everything we experience is filtered through and corrupted by it. For example, I have known many women who feel worthless. They can never seem to be good enough or measure up to some impossible invisible standard. Why? Because worthless has become their identity. At one time they experienced feeling worthlessness in a circumstance or situation. Now, they no longer feel or experience worthlessness, they *are* worthless. They cannot receive a compliment without qualifying why it can't be true or that the praise belongs to someone else. This response is a deflection. Why? Because they believe they are worthless. It has become an identity. They cannot accept praise or anything of value as their own. When God gives a gift of any kind – mercy, grace, love, forgiveness, a calling, prophetic promises, finances – they can't receive it because, in their understanding, they are worthless, and unworthy. They say things like, "I don't deserve it. He would not really give me this. It can't really be true. If you really knew who I was underneath this nice smile and these clothes, you would not compliment me because you would know that I'm worthless. This must be meant for someone else."

Do you see how that works?

If grief becomes an identity then we always expect the worst and never expect any good. David sat down among the people and grieved until he had no strength. He was authentic about his emotions and his experience. But he did not stop there.

David Strengthened Himself

"And David was greatly distressed, for the people spoke of stoning him, because all the people were bitter in soul, each for his sons and daughters. *But David* [emphasis mine] strengthened himself in the LORD his God." (Verse 6).

Second, David *strengthened himself in the Lord.*

This is a key to enduring in trial! Earlier we discussed that the author of Samuel, inspired by the Holy Spirit, has used words

23

purposefully in recording this true story. Consider the words, *but David*. The word *but* is so important. Scripture assures us that David was greatly distressed. His mighty men, his friends, want to stone him. There is great emotion everywhere – b*ut David*. It is a sign to us. What we would expect to happen does not. David does not react in retaliation toward the mighty men.

Why? This *but* represents that moment in time where we all can make a choice before we respond. It is our *response-ability*. There is always a moment, in every situation that we face and every conversation that we have, when we have to make a choice. The result of that choice is our response. Whether we make the choice consciously or unconsciously, our response belongs to us. We must own it, along with the outcome. It's a part of the freedom we have been given in Christ (Phil. 2:12-13). God has His part and we have ours. We have personal power and freedom to make decisions that will affect the outcome of this whole situation. David had the freedom to choose, just as the Amalekites, Saul, and his mighty men did, and each one of us does too. The outcome of our freedom to choose is never an isolated event. It always affects the situation and the lives of others.

David chose to look to God for strength and encouragement. He took his eyes off the situation and put them on God. His choice reveals his faith, his understanding of his spiritual identity, and his calling. It helps him maintain his identity. David knew he was a beloved son of God. He knew he was loved. He knew he had a prophecy. He knew he was called, anointed and appointed by God. He knew he was not an orphan and he was not left alone. He responded to this crisis the way he had learned to respond in all circumstances – by turning to the God he *knew*. His choice reveals his trust in God.

David's God

David drew on his personal experience and relationship with God. What was his personal experience? In his own words,

"Lord, how many are my foes! How many rise up against me! Many are saying of me, "God will not deliver him". But you, Lord, are a shield around me, my glory, the One who lifts my head high. I call out to the Lord, and he answers me from his holy mountain. I lie down and sleep; I wake again, because the Lord sustains me. I will not fear though tens of thousands assail me on every side. Arise, Lord! Deliver me, my God! Strike all my enemies on the jaw; break the teeth of the wicked. From the Lord comes deliverance. May your blessing be on your people." Psalm 3:1-7 (written by David).

David's God was sovereign. David's God was a God of covenant and his promises could not be broken. David's God was good. David's God was compassionate. David's God was loving. David's God was merciful. David's God was gracious. David's God was listening. David's God was speaking. David's God was a strong tower. David's God was powerful and mighty to deliver. David's God was for him. He was not sleeping at any moment of David's life, but He was ready and willing and able to stand with him and go with him and win the victory for him. *This is* David's God!

David did not take the circumstances and apply them to God making a judgment about his character or his ability. He took his experience, his intimate knowledge of God and applied them to the circumstances. His circumstances did not change the way he saw God, his God changed the way he saw circumstances.

It is often all in how you look at it. There comes a time for all of us when the words of God need to become an experience of God. We talk so much about knowing God, but we can't settle for just knowing about God. We can memorize the entire Bible,

25

but until the words become our personal experience, until we encounter God in the word, it will not change our lives. The events of our lives that are sent by the enemy to tear us down will dethrone our God in our lives if we do not know God by experience and faith. Our God is greater, our God is good, our God is for us, our God is with us, and our God loves us. We are God's treasured possessions. It says in Scripture we belong to God.

I don't know about you, but I want to come to the place where my threatening, frightening, or painful circumstances do not emasculate, disempower, dethrone, or belittle my God, but rather my great God emasculates, belittles, disempowers and dethrones my circumstances along with the enemy that designed them. *God* has not changed. Encourage yourself in the Lord. Put him in remembrance. "Draw near to God, and he will draw near to you." says James, in Chapter 4.

I don't know about you, but I want to come to the place where my threatening, frightening, or painful circumstances do not emasculate, disempower, dethrone, or belittle my God, but rather my great God emasculates, belittles, disempowers and dethrones my circumstances along with the enemy that designed them.

David Inquired of the Lord

"And David said to Abiathar the priest, the son of Ahimelech, 'Bring me the ephod.' So Abiathar brought the ephod to David. And David inquired of the LORD, 'Shall I pursue after this band? Shall I overtake them?' " (Verses 8-9).

26

Third, David called for the priest and he inquired of the Lord. All throughout the history of David's life, at key moments, he inquired of the Lord. In this moment as well, David chose to go to God for direction. It was his practice. He had established this habit in easier times. He had decided and made it his practice to live from every word that proceeded from the mouth of God.

It is difficult in a crisis to put into practice something that has not been established in peace.

I was a labor and delivery nurse for years before God called me to full time ministry. Countless times I faced crisis situations involving life and death. In those moments, the training and instruction I had received and practiced regularly came into play. The practice was preparation for the times of crisis so that when I faced a life and death situation, I had an arsenal of knowledge and skill to make good decisions and save lives.

David made an excellent choice. The extreme pressure of the moment did not change David's priorities. He was able to rise above the swirling emotion, the confusion, the distractions, the pressure, the anger, and the bitterness, to take the time to see the situation from God's perspective. He understood that the most important and most needed thing was a willingness to let God speak into the situation and not make a decision on his own. He needed revelation and guidance regarding God's will and perspective in the situation. He needed God's revelatory word.

He brings his questions to God. Notice that David does not ask why this happened. He does not spend his time asking how God could let it happen. He asks how to gain victory in the situation.

> *Notice, David does not ask why this happened. He does not spend his time asking how God could let it happen. He asks how to gain victory in the situation.*

Jeremiah 33:3 instructs us to call on God and He will show us great and mighty things we have not known. Why is this important? The great and mighty things are referring to revelation. Revelation is something only God can give. It is not something we can know by research and education. It is not something we can know out of our own great personal experience, knowledge and wisdom. It can only be known when God reveals it. It is something only He knows and cannot be found by any means except by revelation from Him. Our God knows each of us intimately because He has called us each by name. He knows the past and the future. He knows what is up ahead and coming our way. He knows what we do not and cannot know. We must go to God for revelation and guidance. When we do, "He will show us great and mighty things that we have not known." (Jeremiah 33:3).

Saul did not wait to hear from God. In a story just prior to Ziklag, he sought a medium. He resorted to witchcraft to find the answers to his questions. It did not work out well for Saul. He went to the wrong source. The source of our information, our guidance and our wisdom, cannot be human wisdom or demonic revelation because the vision will always be limited. To receive light, the source can never be darkness. The enemy has a plan for our lives. He is happy to offer a counterfeit every single time. It may even seem right and true. Think about it. When Satan tempted Jesus in the wilderness, he used Scripture. Satan is a liar and he has been a liar from the beginning. He cannot offer anything but lies and counterfeits. Our source *must* be God.

The Lord, through the priest, answers David with a command and a promise of the future. Victory belongs to David. God's word never returns void. David gave God the last word.

Who is getting the last word in our situations?

David Obeyed

"He [God] answered him, "Pursue, for you shall surely overtake and shall surely rescue." *So David set out. . . ."* [emphasis mine]. (Verses 8-9a).

Lastly, David obeyed God. David chose to take God at His word and pursue the enemy.

This is so important. David had strengthened and encouraged himself in the Lord. He had inquired of the Lord and heard a good word. However, if David had never acted on the word given, the promised outcome would not come to pass. Hearing and obeying can never be separated. God's word is powerful. His direction leads to success. He commands and the creative redemptive power of His word in our lives is appropriated when we obey. Through obedience we receive the prophesied outcome.

Some of us have experienced this with our own adult children. They come to inquire of us because they are in a troublesome situation or crisis. They are seeking wisdom and direction. We give them wise counsel because we have been there, done that. We know what they are going through. We have wisdom for how to get out of the tough situation. They say, "Oh Mom and Dad that was so good, thank you so much. I so appreciate it. I get it now and I know how to get out of this." Then they leave your house and do not follow the advice. And what happens? Nothing. Why? Because if nothing changes – *nothing* changes.

In scripture, hearing implies an acceptance and follow-through in action on what is heard. Therefore, a word heard finds its completion in action. Action in agreement with the heard word is obedience. Disobedience is either no action, incomplete action, or inappropriate action (i.e. action that is not in agreement with the word). God's word is powerful. When He speaks a prophetic revelatory word, we need to act on it. Obedience to His word allows all the power of that word to be appropriated in our lives. Isaiah says that God's word never returns void, it will always do what it was sent out to do. We come into agreement with that word through obedience. Coming into agreement means that our behavior, the choices that we make, and the actions that we take are directed by that word.

David obeyed God. He did not hesitate, negotiate, or shrink back. His obedience released the power of the word and promise. God's will on earth, as it is in heaven, would be done in his life.

Reversal and Recovery

David recovered all.

He recovered everything and more. In twelve days he would step onto the throne and receive his promised, prophesied crown. David's choices, his unwavering faith revealed by his response at Ziklag, allowed the power of God's word to be released bringing God's plan for his life to fullness. He endured and received the promise. He became the promised, prophesied King. The *crisis* gave way to a *crown*.

Jesus knew the greatest reversal of all was coming through him. He faced the cross enduring to the fulfillment of the promise of God. The works of darkness would never prevail. The gift of redemption and the empowerment of the

Holy Spirit would be available to all. The lepers would be cleansed, the lame healed, blind eyes opened, and the oppressed set free. The Enemy thought the cross was the game changer – he hadn't understood how much.

Stay the course! Do not throw away your confidence in Jesus – in who He is and what He has said. Endure and receive the promise! Make your choices count toward moving forward!

> *David's choices, his unwavering faith revealed by his response at Ziklag, allowed the power of God's word to be released bringing God's plan for his life to fullness. He endured and received the promise. He became the promised, prophesied King. The crisis gave way to a crown.*

Part II
The Rest of the Story

Introduction

In the big picture, we remember that Samuel is a book about socio-political and religious transition for the nation of Israel. David's Journey, his choices and actions, were going to affect history.

We too are living in a time of historic socio-political and religious shifts. Our choices and actions, as God's people and ambassadors of Christ, are going to affect history. I believe we have an unprecedented opportunity to influence history if we will grab hold of our identity in Christ, stand in our call and obey God's every word. We have a part to play in this time of transition and the decisions we make as we face our Ziklag moments will make all the difference in the world for our lives, the lives of those who follow us, and the lives of those we are yet to influence.

In Facing Ziklag Part I, we focused on David and his responses in the moment of crisis. But the story does not end there. Here, in Part II, we get the rest of the story. David has responded to the crisis and inquired of the Lord. He acts on the word of The Lord. He has made many choices as to how he would personally respond to the crisis, and now we follow him as he follows through. He deals wisely with the four *E's*: *Err, Egyptians, Exhaustion, and Extra.*

I Samuel 30: 8-31

"And David said to Abiathar the priest, the son of Ahimelech, 'Bring me the ephod.' So Abiathar brought the ephod to David. And David inquired of the LORD, 'Shall I pursue after this band? Shall I overtake them?' He answered him, 'Pursue, for you shall surely overtake and shall surely rescue.' So David set out, and the six hundred men who were with him, and they came to the brook Besor, where those who were left behind stayed. But David pursued, he and four hundred men. Two hundred stayed behind, who were too exhausted to cross the brook Besor.

They found an Egyptian in the open country and brought him to David. And they gave him bread and he ate. They gave him water to drink, and they gave him a piece of a cake of figs and two clusters of raisins. And when he had eaten, his spirit revived, for he had not eaten bread or drunk water for three days and three nights. And David said to him, 'To whom do you belong? And where are you from?' He said, 'I am a young man of Egypt, servant to an Amalekite, and my master left me behind because I fell sick three days ago. We had made a raid against the Negeb of the Cherethites and against that which belongs to Judah and against the Negeb of Caleb, and we burned Ziklag with fire.' And David said to him, 'Will you take me down to this band?' And he said, 'Swear to me by God that you will not kill me or deliver me into the hands of my master, and I will take you down to this band.'

And when he had taken him down, behold, they were spread abroad over all the land, eating and drinking and dancing, because of all the great spoil they had taken from the land of the Philistines and from the land of Judah. And David struck them down from twilight until the evening of the next day, and not a man of them escaped, except four hundred young men, who mounted camels and fled. David recovered all that the Amalekites had taken, and David rescued his two wives. Nothing was missing, whether small or great, sons or daughters, spoil or anything that had been taken. David brought back all. David also captured all the flocks and herds, and the people drove the livestock before him, and said, 'This is David's spoil.'

Then David came to the two hundred men who had been too exhausted to follow David, and who had been left at the brook Besor. And they went out to meet David and to meet the people who were with him. And when David came near to the people he greeted them. Then all the wicked and worthless fellows among the men who had gone with David said, 'Because they did not go with us, we will not give them any of the spoil that we have recovered, except that each man may lead away his wife and children, and depart.' But David said, 'You shall not do so, my brothers, with what the LORD has given us. He has preserved us and given into our hand the band that came against us. Who would listen to you in this matter? For as his share is who goes down into the battle, so shall his share be who stays by the baggage. They shall share alike.' And he made it a statute and a rule for Israel from that day forward to this day.

When David came to Ziklag, he sent part of the spoil to his friends, the elders of Judah, saying, 'Here is a present for you from the spoil of the enemies of the LORD.' It was for those in Bethel, in Ramoth of the Negeb, in Jattir, in Aroer, in Siphmoth, in Eshtemoa, in Racal, in the cities of the Jerahmeelites, in the cities of the Kenites, in Hormah, in Bor-ashan, in Athach, in Hebron, for all the places where David and his men had roamed."

Dealing with *Err*

Let's recapture the scene. David was fleeing Saul, the reigning king. He was a fugitive with a reputation for being a courageous and victorious warrior. In the wake of returning to Ziklag to find their homes burned and their families taken hostage to a cruel enemy, David's mighty men return to their old identity.

The words used to describe their state of being are the same words used to describe the condition of their character when they first came to David. Samuel records that the men who were bitter of soul – in debt and discontented – gathered to David. They became his army. They became David's mighty men, the army of the prophesied king of Israel. They fought, ate, drank, lived, followed and submitted to him. They loved him. But, in the face of Ziklag, their grief and despair caused them to turn on their friend and leader and turn from their true identity. They *erred*.

They resorted to their old life, turning from the Kingdom journey. In their distress, they reacted. We are left to wonder if all is lost.

But David. David did not follow his men; he led them.

> "And David inquired of the LORD, 'Shall I pursue after this band? Shall I overtake them?' He answered him, 'Pursue, for you shall surely overtake and shall surely rescue.' So David set out, and the six hundred men who were with him . . ."

There are times when the people around us, or the people we lead, come to the place where they succumb to their circumstances and the deception brought by the enemy. They react in their emotion. They cannot see the way forward and so turn backward. They *err* – make bad choices, wrong choices, and even betray our friendship. They turn from their Kingdom journey which was the goal of the enemy from the beginning. In those times, we must recognize that we have been positioned in their lives to lead them out from there. We are there to remind them of who they really are and how far they have come, and to model the way forward.

Whether we are in formal positions of leadership or not, we have a responsibility towards one another. Leaders or not, we are part of a community in which we stand as equals, not over and above one another. Maybe today I am able to respond in faith and stand in my true identity in Christ to lead the way forward. Maybe tomorrow I will need leading.

Even right now, right where you are, there are those who are waiting and watching how you will respond to the challenges in your life and it will make all the difference for redemption and recovery in their journey.

David's response redeemed the situation and recovered the identity of his men. He led them forward, out of their rebellion, and toward the Kingdom. As he leads, they regain their identity as *mighty men of valor*. We know this because in the rest of 1 Samuel, as well as in II Samuel, Chronicles and Kings, we read all about the exploits of David's mighty men. They may have turned for a moment, being overcome by their emotion, but they did not lose their way. David led them out.

This is so important to understand. When we face crisis and respond more as David's men than as David, all is not lost. We are still who God says we are. The gifts and callings of God are irrevocable.

Our God is a God of redemption and recovery. Look up. Look to Jesus, the author and finisher of our faith, who for the joy set before Him, endured the cross, scorning its shame. Jesus has already recovered everything. He has already plundered the enemy's camp. We all come out ahead. We are the head and not the tail. We can look for who He has placed in our lives to lead us. Then follow their lead. God has not left us as orphans nor has He left us without a way forward.

For Leaders

As leaders, a Ziklag moment is a trial and test of what we know to be true of God and His word. Responding with faith and wisdom not only allows us to move forward toward receiving the promises of God, but also leads others there. Part of our responsibility to those under our influence is to help them discover and mature in their identity in Christ. One man, David, led six hundred men out of their backslidden state. Not by reprimanding, guilting, manipulating, accusing or punishing them in the name of accountability and discipleship. He did it by staying true to his way of living before God, true to his understanding of who God is and what God has said, and true to obeying God in dire circumstance in full public view. In this way his leadership was sealed among them.

Are you looking to seal your leadership among the people with whom God has placed you? It is not found in their response to you – it is found in your responses to God amid every life circumstance, especially the tough ones. It is also found in your response to others.

Dealing with *Egyptians*

Have you ever noticed that God often sends direction in unexpected ways?

He never seems to spell things out all the way, in the kind of detail we would like, when we need direction. This is important to remember. Our obedience cannot depend on having all the details. The Lord told David to "pursue." He did not say, "Go right at that big oak tree, cross the field and behind the dome shaped rock, about three miles from there, you will find those you are after." Notice David's response. Like Abraham before him, who went out not knowing the details of where he was going. David went out trusting God would show him as he went.

> *Our obedience cannot depend on having all the details.*

"They found an Egyptian in the open country and brought him to David." (Verse 11)

Remember, David and his men had just traveled three days, suffered a great shock and tragedy without refreshment, rest or provisions. Now, they set out again in obedience to a very general directional word and the promise of victory. There is no mention of how long David and his men had already been pursuing the enemy at this point in the narrative. There is also no mention of having any clue about the whereabouts of their enemy. The only mention is that suddenly, while pursuing in the open country, the men find an *Egyptian*.

When they found the Egyptian, he was half dead. They could not have known he had the intel they needed. Perhaps they recognized he was a stranger, in a strange place at a strange time. Perhaps they could ascertain that he was a captured slave just as their wives and children had become. In any case, this was an outsider, a slave, a sick and dying man, left along the way side, that they happened to stumble upon. Coincidence? Not likely in God's economy.

"And they gave him bread and he ate. . . . And when he had eaten, his spirit revived, for he had not eaten bread or drunk water for three days and three nights. And David said to him, 'To whom do you belong? And where are you from?' He said, 'I am a young man of Egypt, servant to an Amalekite, and my master left me behind because I fell sick three days ago. We had made a raid against the Negeb of the Cherethites and against that which belongs to Judah and against the Negeb of Caleb, and we burned Ziklag with fire.' " (Verses 11-15).

David's men came upon this Egyptian and they brought him to David. How did David respond? The scripture does not specify that David knew this was a sign from God or any such thing; but he had already demonstrated from the beginning that he was responding with wisdom, in faith and openness, to God's leading. Seeing the man, he meets his physical needs first. Then, he asked questions to which he received the revelation needed to complete the mission and realize the prophetic promise of victory.

The point here is simple. The help we need – the direction we are looking for – often comes in a form we do not expect; a person we feel is an outsider; an interruption along the way that takes our time and resources. In those moments it is a good practice to ask questions. What is God doing here? Why is this person introduced into this situation at this time? What am I supposed to get out of this, learn from this, and discover in this?

> "And David said to him, 'Will you take me down to this band?' And he said, 'Swear to me by God that you will not kill me or deliver me into the hands of my master, and I will take you down to this band.' " (Verse 15)

If David had treated the Egyptian with disdain or harshness, would he have received the information he needed? Possibly. However, would David have engendered the trust of the man necessary to gain partnership? Only the Egyptian knew the way forward. God allowed an outsider and age-old enemy of Israel (remember Moses?), to be the one person who could lead David into position to gain the promise.

How we treat all people matters, not just those under our influence. Outsiders, foreigners, difficult people, even old enemies may be our next ally or God's appointed messenger. They may have the answer we need most at a critical moment. God may be placing an *Egyptian* in our path right now, during a most difficult trial, with the revelation we need to recover.

They may not look like much and may not be in any condition we think is worthy. They may not be someone we feel has much significance, but if we jump to judgment and do not discern God's hand in the situation, we may miss what they have to offer. It is so important to be sensitive along the way to what God may be doing. We must remember that He is always working. We must remain open to His ways and deal well with *Egyptians*.

> *How we treat all people matters; not just those under our influence.*

Dealing with *Exhaustion*

Why is it that in our culture we find it so hard to rest? The Book of Hebrews speaks of entering God's rest. It is a rest that comes by embracing a confident trust in God. Can we trust God with our lives? Can we trust Him with the journey, the outcomes, the call and all the promises when we come to a place like the brook Besor, as did David and his men?

We are living in such a crucial time. We must know how to rest – how to not come under *a pressure to perform*. I love what Henri Nouwen states in his book on leadership. He writes, "Jesus refused to be a stuntman."[2] We all, at times, go through things that have gone on and on and on – beyond the boundaries

---

[2]Henri J. M. Nouwen, *In the Name of Jesus: Reflections on Christian Leadership*, (Crossroads, 1998), 38.

of our physical and emotional strength. We find ourselves *exhausted.*

> *"Jesus refused to be a stuntman." Henri J.M. Nouwen*

David is leader, future king, and a type of Christ. The way he responds to his men when they are exhausted is one of the most poignant and beautiful lessons found in scripture. We hear the echo of our Great Shepherd, Jesus himself, who says, "Come to me, all who labor and are heavy laden, and I will give you rest." (Matthew 11:28)

> ". . . they came to the brook Besor. . . . But David pursued, he and four hundred men. Two hundred stayed behind, who were too exhausted to cross the brook Besor." (Verses 9-10).

Picture the scene.

David and his men are pursuing the enemy according to the Word of the Lord. They are trusting God's word to be victorious in taking back their wives, children, and possessions. At this point in the story, they had come from a long journey on foot, having dealt with a dangerous political situation. They arrived home to find complete destruction. Their homes were burned, and their families had been taken captive. They are in crisis.
David seeks God and hears the word of the Lord to pursue with a promise of recovering all that had been lost.

Without rest, without restocking provisions, without details about how far they would have to go or what kind of battle they would face, they *pursue*. Now, they come to the brook Besor. Scholars say it was more than a bubbling brook and likely presented a treacherous crossing. Two hundred men decide they will stay behind. They were exhausted. They were the *exhausted*

44

ones. They were so weary they could not cross the Brook. In the original Hebrew language, the *exhausted ones* can be translated as the weak, the tired, the frightened, or the failed.

After the battle and subsequent victory, David and his men return.

> ". . . David came to the two hundred men who had been too exhausted to follow David, and who had been left at the brook Besor. And they went out to meet David and to meet the people who were with him. . . . Then all the wicked and worthless fellows among the men who had gone with David said, 'Because they did not go with us, we will not give them any of the spoil that we have recovered, except that each man may lead away his wife and children and depart.' " (Verses 21-22).

From the perspective of David's men who went to battle, those who stayed behind did not deserve the spoils. They did not take the risk. They did not pay the cost that the rest of the men had. Surely, they deserve nothing since they were weak, tired, frightened, and failed when it counted most.

Isn't this what we fear people will think if we stop to rest, or admit we are too weary to go on? Are we afraid others will think we have become the weak, the tired, the frightened, and the failed? Is this what we ourselves think about those who become the weak, the tired, the frightened, and the failed who stay behind in the journey?

The attitude, though often unspoken, sounds like this, "Surely they don't deserve anything. They were weak when it counted most. They can stay as part of the church, but they should not think to participate in anything meaningful. After all, they cannot be trusted when it really counts. They can stick around to enjoy all that the rest of us are doing for the Kingdom. They should be grateful for that." I have encountered this attitude. Maybe you have too.

The men who went out to battle pushed through the weariness, recovered the people and the plunder, then judged and pronounced sentence on those who stayed behind. Scripture calls them worthless and wicked men. They are judged for judging. In Matthew 7:1-2, Jesus said:

> "Judge not, that you may not be judged. For with the judgment you pronounce, you will be judged, and with the measure you use it will be measured to you."

How did David respond?

> "But David said, 'You shall not do so, my brothers, with what the LORD has given us. He has preserved us and given into our hand the band that came against us. . . . For as his share is who goes down into the battle, so shall his share be who stays by the baggage. They shall share alike.' " (Verses 23-25).

David's response is contrasted, once again, with his men who are called *worthless and wicked*. The author is making a critical point. He wants readers in every generation to understand that David is righteous and representing God in this matter. All will share in the spoils – those who stay with the baggage and those who fight the battles.

Why is this important? We are to understand that what qualifies us to receive the benefits of the King and His Kingdom is simply membership in the community. Every member of the community is to be cared for, blessed, loved and counted worthy of God's blessing and promise. What gives us membership? It is *relationship* with God, not our performance.

David is a type of Christ acting on behalf of God. The Kingdom is not based on works. It is based on God's word and God's love. When you and I are exhausted, and we stay behind for a time to heal, recover, and rest we do not forfeit the benefits of the Kingdom. It is a religious spirit that wants to punish and disqualify people when they have encountered crisis and difficult times and can't participate for a time.

> *The Kingdom is not based on works. It is based on God's word and God's love. When you and I are exhausted, and we stay behind for a time to heal, recover, and rest we do not forfeit the benefits of the Kingdom.*

If you are exhausted because of the trial that is upon you, you are not counted out or down for the count. If you are weak in this hour, you are not discredited. If you are frightened by what you are facing, you are not disgraced. If your strength has failed, you are not disqualified, dishonored and condemned. Paul said there is no condemnation for those who are in Christ Jesus. The enemy is a liar, a schemer and an accuser. As the Church we must learn to love one another and honor those who stay with the baggage being too exhausted to cross over and fight at times.

The mighty men who stayed behind in their exhaustion were still mighty men. Exhaustion did not mean they forfeited their identity. Their identity, position, and authority were not lost because they had need of rest. David honored them. He did not label them according to human limitation. He honored their place in the community of God and invited them to share in what the Kingdom had to offer. One day they would fight again as Scripture attests. One day they would stand fully recovered and mighty in battle to once again face the enemy and fight for the Kingdom.

Being exhausted is not a disqualification for service in the Kingdom of God but having a judging and condemning attitude toward people just might be.

Being exhausted was not a disqualifier for two hundred of David's mighty men. They were still mighty though they were weary. So it is for those of us who are exhausted. There is a restoration coming. Ziklag was not the end of the story. It was a shift that signaled the end of a long season of transition and the beginning of a new era.

May I speak directly to those of you reading this right now who have become exhausted – who have been hit with such a crisis or hard times that you have needed to stay behind awhile in your journey? Maybe you see other people moving forward and it hurts. It leaves you feeling left behind and disqualified. Maybe you feel you will never recover to take your place in the Kingdom. Maybe you feel you just do not have what it takes and are just not as gifted or as capable as those around you.

The Lord would say to you right now, "*Take the time to rest and recover. You are not disqualified.*" Let the Holy Spirit come to comfort, heal, and enable you".

I also want to speak to those who have felt judged and condemned as weak and worthless by others, especially by leaders in the church. I repent on behalf of any leader who made you feel disqualified and condemned because of the difficult place you were in at that time in your life. I ask you to forgive us all. It was wrong. It never should have happened. If Jesus does not condemn you for being weary, but says "Come to me, I will give you rest." then leaders should do likewise. You have permission, given by God, to be a significant part of what God is doing even if for a time you need to stay behind to rest awhile.

As a Pastor in the Church, I bless you. I bless you in your rest. I bless you if you are frightened. I bless you if you are weary. I bless you if your strength has failed along the way. I break off any word curse or condemnation that the enemy has brought to you, in Jesus name, and I release a recharging and refreshing over you.

David was indeed a wise and righteous leader. Oh, that we all would deal so graciously and wisely with those given us to steward! When those around us are weary and exhausted, may we give them permission to rest without withholding honor, love, or blessing.

Dealing with *Extra*

This last point is simple and short, but no less significant. As people of the Kingdom, we must know how to deal with extra – meaning abundance.

> "When David came to Ziklag, he sent part of the spoil to his friends, the elders of Judah, saying, 'Here is a present for you from the spoil of the enemies of the LORD.' . . . for all the places where David and his men had roamed." (Verses 26-31).

David recovered everything taken by the enemy and more. The Amalekites had not only raided Ziklag but other cities and camps as well. They had taken much more than the wives, possessions, and livestock belonging to David. David recovered far more than he lost. Unlike his men who decided only those who went to battle should share in the abundance recovered, David decided all in the community would enjoy what God provided in the spoils. Then David went even further, he shared the spoil with those considered part of the family of God in surrounding areas.

So what point is the author trying to make? There are several.

David was politically shrewd in building alliances by sharing the spoils. David was generous of heart recognizing the battle is never won alone. David was revealing himself as a benevolent king under whose rule a people prosper. He was acting with vision for the future, expanding his influence and network

There is something else. David sends a present to his friends and the elders of Judah. The Hebrew word for *present* in this passage is the word for *blessing*. David acted out of His identity as a son of God and prophesied King. The blessing of God on his life was to have an outflow of blessing to others. God could trust David with abundant resources. Over and over, his responses reveal his faithfulness and sensitivity to God's word and God's will. David used the blessing of God to further God's plan and make known the blessings of being in a covenant relationship with God. In being blessed, David blessed.

> *Abundance and prosperity are a blessing from God. Abundance and prosperity can be a serious test of our spiritual identity and heart attitude.*

Abundance and prosperity are a blessing from God. Abundance and prosperity can be a serious test of our spiritual identity and heart attitude. David models for us the right attitude, which is gratitude. He models for us the right posture, which is stewardship and servanthood. Lastly, David models for us how to deal with *extra* as a son or daughter of God, which is to build the Kingdom and bless others.

The Conclusion of the Matter

Twelve days later, David's season as a fugitive in exile ended. Twelve days later, David was crowned king. He stepped into the promised prophesied kingship. The attack at Ziklag was not only one of the most difficult and painful of his life, but also the most pivotal. His responses made all the difference. He demonstrated a life lived by faith in God. At each critical juncture, he remained faithful and true to His God.

Throughout history, God's people face intense testing and trials in the transitional moments just before the fulfillment of God's promises. Understanding the choices behind David's responses to the crisis encourages us to be prepared to face our own Ziklag and see every *crisis* become a *crown.*

We are living in a time of historic socio-political and religious shifts. We have a part to play in this time. The decisions we make as we face our Ziklag moments will make all the difference in the world for our lives, for the lives of those who follow us, and for the lives of those we are yet to influence. Therefore, stand fast. Be brave. Move forward. God is with us. The Holy Spirit will fill and empower you.

Below is a prayer declaration for your use in a Ziklag moment. God Bless you in your journey.

In the Name of Jesus Christ of Nazareth, I declare that no weapon formed against me shall prosper. I stand under the shed blood of Jesus Christ and in His name. I will not be moved. Satan, you have no authority over me and my household. I declare the name and Lordship of Jesus over my life and all that concerns me and I bind on earth the tactics, schemes, devices, and plans of the enemy to take captive my mind, heart, soul and spirit, and I violently say NO! I silence you in the name of Jesus and break your power. I overcome by the blood of Jesus and the word of my testimony of Christ who lived, died, and rose again on my behalf, and to Whom I belong. Father, I declare that You alone are the lifter of my head, the healer of my body, the deliverer of my life, the savior of my soul. I am the head and not the tail, I am the victor not the victim, I am not defeated but I am more than a conqueror in Christ Jesus because He who is in me is greater than he who is in the world therefore I will not give in, back down, lie down, shrink back, turn back, roll over, play dead, or succumb to the lies and the counterfeits of the enemy.

I will stand my ground, step up, move forward and advance on the enemy's camp and bring back the spoils, displacing the work of darkness with the light of Jesus Christ. Father, give me courage and strength and stamina in this hour. Fortify my mind, soul, body and spirit. Give me eyes to see and ears to hear what Your Spirit is saying that I may follow and obey all that You command. Give me the peace that surpasses all understanding and make me able to trust in You alone. Empower me afresh; bring to my remembrance all that You have done for me that I may stand in the testimony of Your goodness and mercy. I worship only You. You are the great and good God. Praise Your name, Lord Jesus. In the mighty, unmatched name of Jesus,

Amen!

FACING ZIKLAG:
TURNING CRISIS INTO CROWNS

Crisis comes to everyone. It is a strategy devised by the enemy to keep you from your God-given destiny and often comes moments before the fulfilment of a prophetic promise. No one is immune. David was only twelve days from becoming king and receiving the crown prophesied to him by Samuel when he faced the events at Ziklag. The enemy hit him hard in a place and in a way he did not expect or anticipate, turning his world upside down. His decisions would be crucial to the outcome.

In this two-part booklet, you will discover how David's choices and response to God during the most pivotal moment in his life make all the difference in turning his crisis in to a crown. Gain the insight, keys, and strategy you need for facing, navigating, and overcoming your own Ziklag moments, with unwavering faith and courage.

The Facing Ziklag Companion Journal is a "must have" to help you work through your own Ziklag moment and move you forward to see your crisis turned into a crown.

 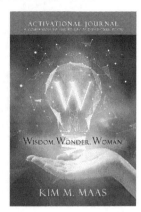

FOUR QUESTIONS WORKBOOK
YOUR STRATEGY FOR MOVING FORWARD

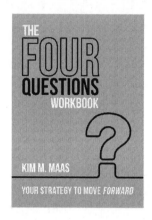

At the end of every season, we have moved from where we were the season before. The question is, have we moved forward?

Ask yourself a few questions. How do you feel when you go to bed each night? Have you accomplished the things that are most important to you? Have you accomplished the things in line with who God says you are and has called you to do? What do you imagine it would feel like to know you accomplished those things for several days in a row? Where would you find yourself if you did them consistently for a whole season?

This is the perfect time to move forward in God's dreams and vision for your life. It's not complicated. It begins with a strategy. Whether it is a new year, or new season, this practical workbook is designed to help you create a strategy for moving forward toward the fulfillment of the dreams and visions God has for your life.

ABOUT DR. KIM MAAS

Dr. Kim Maas is an international speaker and the Founder of Kim Maas Ministries, Inc. She has trained and equipped churches, ministries, and individuals to operate in the gift of prophecy in several nations and the United States. After a radical encounter with the Holy Spirit March 22, 1994, Kim left her twenty-two year nursing career to serve God full time. Her passion is to inspire, encourage and equip God's people to move forward toward fulfilling the call of God on their lives. This passion comes through in her preaching, leadership, writing, and everyday life. She is the president and C.E.O. of KIM MAAS MINISTRIES, Inc. and the founder and director of Women of Our Time (WOOT). In addition to speaking, preaching, and writing, she served as a pastor in the local church for over 12 years before becoming a full time itinerant minister. Kim earned a Doctorate in Ministry at United Theological Seminary and a Master of Divinity at King's University. Kim and her husband Mike live in Moorpark, CA. They have three grown children and five grandchildren.

For more information about Dr. Kim Maas or to invite her to speak at your next event visit: kimmaas.com

To follow her on twitter: @pkmaas
Or, write Kim at: hello@kimmaas.com

Dr. Kim Maas
P.O. Box 271
Moorpark, CA 93020

Made in the USA
Monee, IL
09 September 2021